MOM! I NEED GLASSES!

by Angelika Wolff

illustrated by Dorothy Hill

Lion Books, Publisher

TO
MICHAEL
AND ALL
OTHER CHILDREN
WHO WEAR
GLASSES

also by Angelika Wolff:
MOM! I BROKE MY ARM!

THIS IS A LION BOOK
Published by Lion Books, Publisher
Scarsdale, New York
Text copyright © by Angelika Wolff
Illustrations copyright © by Dorothy Hill
Library of Congress Catalog Card Number 74-112648
ISBN: 0-87460-139-8
Printed and Bound in the United States.

This little book for children performs an extremely useful service—the elimination of fear of the unknown and of the misinformation received from playmates and friends.

Children fear the dark examination room, the use of drops and the consequent blurring of vision, and the manipulation of the eyelids.

These problems are adequately dealt with by the author and will be greatly appreciated by all eye doctors whose burdens will now be lightened.

Samuel L. Saltzman, M.D., F.A.C.S.

Samuel L. Saltzman, M.D., F.A.C.S.

"Jump, Susan, jump!" Lisa and Ellen, Susan's two friends, swung the pink jump rope back and forth.

"It's your turn, Susan," said Ellen. "Jump in."

Seven-year-old Susan took a deep breath. She really didn't like to jump rope. She was always afraid to jump in, but she would never tell that to Ellen. She shut her eyes tightly and jumped.

"You missed," laughed Ellen. "You always miss."

Susan pulled up her pink-and-white striped socks. "Let's play something else," she said. "This isn't any fun."

Lisa took a red ball from her shorts pocket. "Catch," she said.

Susan tried, but she missed. The ball was so blurred. She thought she had reached for it, but she hadn't.

"Throw it to me," said Ellen. "I'm a good catcher."

Lisa tossed the ball to Ellen. "You can be the monkey in the middle," she said to Susan. "Here, monkey. Catch, monkey."

Susan ran back and forth between the two girls. "No fair," she said, as the ball soared over her head. "How tall do you think I am?"

Finally, after what seemed like hours, Susan caught the ball and Ellen became the monkey.

Susan rubbed her eyes. It was very hot and she felt tired.

"I wonder what time it is," she asked, but none of the girls had a watch.

"My mother will call us from the window when it's time for us to come up," said Lisa.

All three girls lived in the same apartment house and had been friends for a long time.

"Let's go to the swings," said Susan. The playground belonged to their apartment building and the girls often spent their afternoons there.

They were lucky to find three empty swings. Susan pumped strongly with her legs and her swing went high up in the air. How good it was not to have to catch a ball or jump over a rope, she thought. She wished she could swing forever. The cool breeze felt soft against her hot face.

"Time to go, girls." Suddenly Susan's mother stood near the swings. "It's almost five o'clock."

The girls stopped the swings slowly. Ellen and Lisa walked ahead of Susan and her mother. "What's for dinner, Mom?" Susan was hungry.

"Hamburgers," said Mrs. Monti, "and string beans and potatoes. And jello for dessert."

"Yummy," said Susan. "Will Daddy be home for dinner?"

"I hope so," said Mrs. Monti. "You know he sometimes works late on Wednesdays. That reminds me—do you have homework for tomorrow?"

Susan nodded. "I have math to do, and reading. Mrs. Johnson wants me to do the math over. I copied the numbers wrong from the board."

"Again?" said Mrs. Monti. "You did that last week, too."

"I know," said Susan. "The numbers are fuzzy sometimes."

"I wonder why," mused Mrs. Monti. Just then the phone rang. Susan's father called to say he was bringing a dinner guest.

"That will be fun," said Mrs. Monti. "Hurry up, Susan, and do your homework. Daddy will be here soon. He is bringing Uncle Phil for dinner."

Uncle Phil was Mr. Monti's partner. They owned a vegetable store on Lexington Avenue.

Susan plugged away at her arithmetic. At home the work was easy. It was only in school that she had trouble. The blackboard was always so far away.

The next morning Susan, Lisa and Ellen walked to school together. They were all in second grade. The girls waited for the light to change from red to green before they crossed the street to go to school.

"Today we have music," said Susan. "I like Mrs. Dowd, don't you?"

Lisa and Ellen agreed. "But math is my favorite," said Ellen. "Did you have to do all that homework over, Susan?"

"Yes," said Susan. "I copied the numbers wrong from the board."

"Why don't you ask Mrs. Johnson to change your seat," said Ellen. "Maybe you can see better in the front row."

"I can see all right," said Susan. "Only sometimes I can't see the numbers on the board."

But Mrs. Johnson thought Ellen's idea very good.

"Joanne," she said, "please change seats with Susan Monti." Joanne sat in the front row. "Maybe now you will have less trouble seeing the board."

Susan felt funny all the way up in the front of the room. But the numbers did look much clearer.

After school, Mrs. Johnson called Susan to the front of the room.

"Susan, did you have your eyes checked in first grade last year?" she asked.

Susan tried hard to remember. "Maybe I was absent," she said.

"That's possible," the teacher agreed. "Anyway, I have written a note to your mother. I think you should go to an eye doctor and have your eyes checked. The eye tests for the second grade won't be held for another month or so, and I don't think you should wait that long."

Susan took the note and put it in her school bag. She bit her lower lip. She didn't want glasses. She thought they were ugly and heavy.

"Did you have a good day, dear?" asked Mrs. Monti, when Susan came home. "How did the math go?"

"All right," said Susan. "Mrs. Johnson gave me a note for you, Mom. Here."

"H'm," said Mrs. Monti. "Maybe Mrs. Johnson is right. My sister wears glasses, and so does Daddy's brother. Sometimes that sort of thing runs in the family."

"What sort of thing?" Susan knew that her aunt and uncle wore glasses, but they were adults and not children.

"Near-sightedness," said Mrs. Monti. "I'm going to call the oculist right now."

"What's an oculist?" asked Susan.

"An eye doctor," answered her mother. She was thumbing through the phone book. "Sugar . . . Sugarman," she said. "Here he is. Stanley Sugarman. That's where Aunt Mildred goes."

"Is he nice?" asked Susan. "What will he do to me?"

Mrs. Monti did not hear her. She was busy dialing. "I want to make an appointment for my daughter, Susan," she said into the phone. "No, she has never seen the doctor before. She can't come before four o'clock because she goes to school."

Mrs. Monti sighed. "That will be fine," she said. "We'll come next Tuesday at four-thirty. Yes, we'll be on time. Thank you."

She hung up the telephone, and turned to Susan. "You can tell Mrs. Johnson that you have an appointment with the eye doctor for next Tuesday. That should take care of things."

Susan nodded blankly. She was worried. Her mother hadn't said whether the eye doctor would hurt her eyes. And what would she look like in glasses?

"Want a snack, dear?" Mrs. Monti opened the refrigerator and poured Susan a glass of milk. "Don't look so scared. I've never met Doctor Sugarman, but with a name like that he must be sweet."

Susan took a sip of milk. She didn't think her mother's joke was funny.

"Will it hurt?" she asked.

"Of course not," said Mrs. Monti. "How can it hurt to have your eyes checked?"

Susan didn't answer. She thought her mother might be wrong.

"I'm going out to play with Lisa and Ellen," she said. "They'll be on the swings."

"Finish your milk." Mrs. Monti said. "And please wear your watch. I want you home at five."

In the playground Susan headed straight for the swings. Ellen and Lisa were playing ball with some other children, but Susan really wanted to be alone.

On the swing it was peaceful and she didn't have to think about eye doctors and glasses.

"Today is Thursday," Susan counted. "In five days I'll go to see Doctor Sugarman. I wonder what he will be like?"

The next day Susan told Mrs. Johnson about her appointment with the eye doctor.

"I'm glad to hear that," said the teacher. "In the meantime, you had better keep your front seat."

"May I move back to my old seat after I've been to the doctor?" asked Susan. She missed sitting with her friends.

"We'll see," said Mrs. Johnson. "We'll see."

Tuesday after school Susan ran all the way home. Her mother was waiting for her. "Hurry up," she said. "Drink your milk quickly, so we won't be late."

"Is it far to the doctor's office?" Susan's stomach was turning somersaults.

"No," said her mother. "It's just a bus ride away."

In the bus Susan looked out of the window. "You know," she told her mother, "I can't read all the street signs. They always look a little hazy."

In a few minutes Susan and her mother got off the bus, and headed for a tall white building.

"This is it," said Mrs. Monti. "See, it says 'Doctor Sugarman' in the window."

"Ring the bell and walk in." Susan read the sign on the green door.

Inside the waiting room sat a young lady in a white uniform.

"You must be Susan Monti," she said. "And this is your mother."

"That's right," said Mrs. Monti. "We were referred here by my sister, Mrs. Mildred Jones."

"Just a moment, please," said the lady at the desk. She pulled out a small white card.

"Now I can write down all the pertinent information," she said to Susan. "Tell me your name, age, and the name of the school you attend."

"I go to P. S. Thirty-nine," said Susan. "My name is Susan Monti and I'm seven and a half years old."

"Fine," said the receptionist. "Have a seat over there on the couch. The doctor will be with you shortly."

Susan and her mother sat down. Susan looked around curiously. Stacks of magazines lay on the coffee table in front of her. A boy with glasses was sitting in one of the big arm chairs. Susan wondered why he wore glasses. The boy was fiddling with a black elastic band.

"I can clip this to my glasses in the back," he said. "Then they won't slide off when I play ball."

"Oh," said Susan. "Do you have to wear them all the time?"

"Sure," said her new friend. "Are you going to get glasses, too?"

"I think so," said Susan. "I've never been here before."

"The first time I was here," said the boy, "the doctor put drops in my eyes. I wonder whether he'll do that to you?"

"I hope not," said Susan, frightened.

"My name is Jamie," said the boy. "I come every six months to get my eyes checked. I'm waiting for my mother. I'm early and she's late."

A buzzer rang twice. "The doctor is free now," said the receptionist. "Mrs. Monti and Susan, you may go in now. It's the first door down the hall."

Susan and her mother walked across the waiting room and down the hall. A pleasant-looking man wearing glasses was smiling cheerfully.

"So you are Susan," he said, "and you are Susan's mother." He shook hands formally with Susan and Mrs. Monti.

"What seems to be the trouble?"

"Susan's teacher suggested that we come, Doctor," said Mrs. Monti. "She says Susan can't see the numbers on the board."

"Sit on this white stool," Dr. Sugarman told Susan. He took a very small flashlight from his jacket pocket and shone it into Susan's eyes. "Now step over here and read this chart for me," he said.

Susan sat down on a different chair. The doctor handed her a black eye cup attached to a long handle. On the wall opposite Susan hung a big chart with letters.

"Cover your right eye with the cup," the doctor told Susan.

He flipped a switch and the chart lit up.

"E," read Susan.

"Good," said Dr. Sugarman. "Now read the next two lines."

"F P T O Z," read Susan.

"Go on," encouraged the doctor.

Susan read the next line and the line below. Then the doctor stopped her.

"Whoa," said Dr. Sugarman. "Read that again, and keep your right eye covered."

"E," read Susan. "D H L."

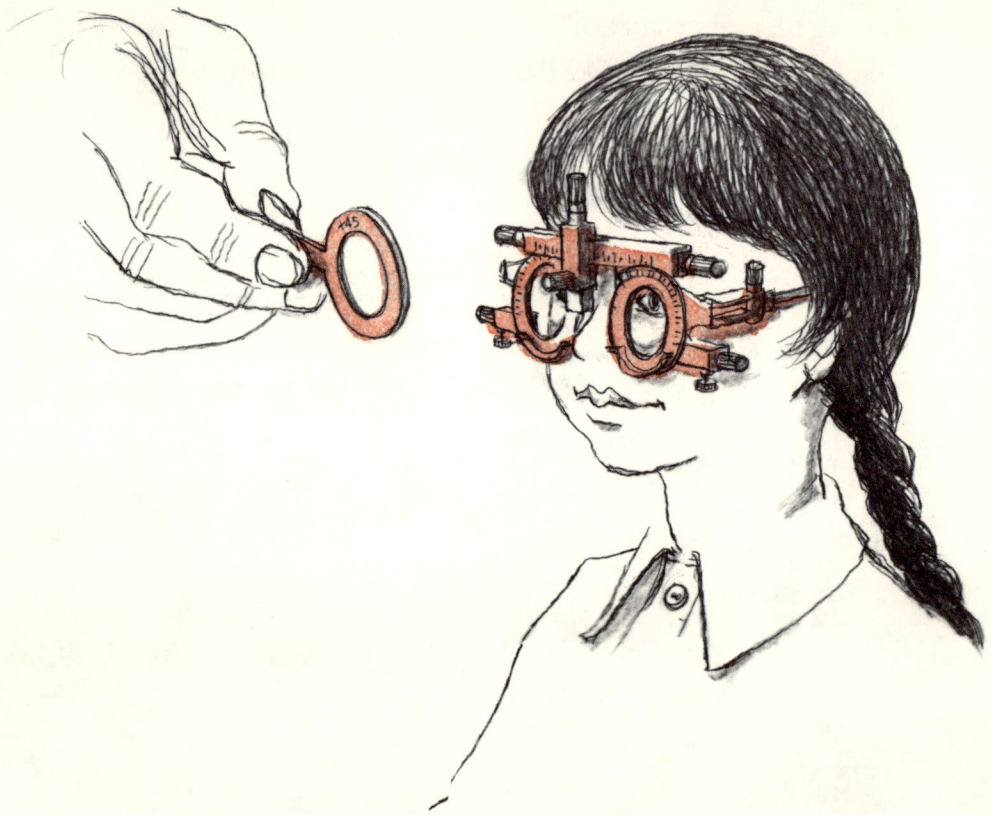

"Hold it," said the doctor. He placed a metal frame without glasses on Susan's nose. "Now," he said, "I am going to put a lens in this frame and you tell me what you see."

"E," read Susan. "D F C Z P."

"Good," said the doctor. "Now let's try the other eye."

Susan covered the left eye with the eye cup and read with the right.

"It's blurred," she said when she came to the sixth line.

"Of course," said Dr. Sugarman. He put a lens in the frame for Susan's right eye. "Now read with both eyes," he said. "How is that?"

"Everything is so clear now," Susan said with delight. "May I keep those glasses?"

Dr. Sugarman laughed. "And what shall I do for the next patient? Don't be in such a hurry." He made some notations on a large sheet of white paper.

"Now let's go into my instrument room," he said to Susan. "I'm sure your mother will excuse us."

In the next room stood many different machines. "Rest your chin in here," said Dr. Sugarman. Susan put her chin on a metal frame. "That's right," said the doctor. "I want to test the reflexes in your eyes."

He shone several kinds of lights into Susan's eyes. "Look up," he said. "Follow my finger with your eyes." Then he switched on a different chart with letters. One side of the chart was green; the other was red.

"Which letters are clearer?" the doctor asked Susan. "The ones on the red chart or on the green one?"

"The green background is much better," said Susan. "The red one is so very bright."

Susan sat very still. She was waiting for the doctor to put drops into her eyes, just the way Jamie had said.

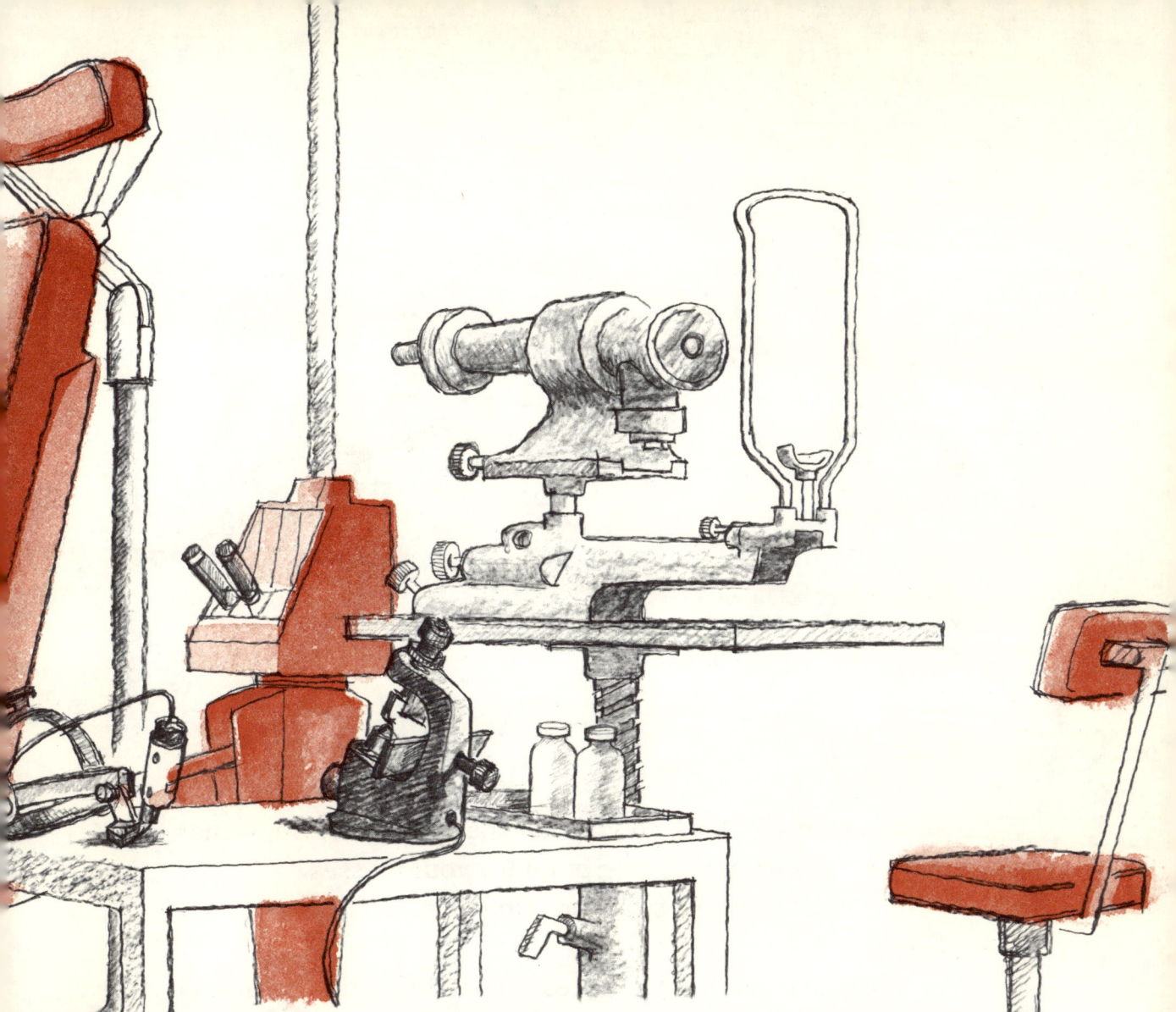

She took a deep breath. "Aren't you going to put drops in my eyes?" she asked. "Jamie said you put drops in his eyes."

Dr. Sugarman smiled. "That boy should mind his own business. No two pairs of eyes are alike. Sometimes I use the drops to put the eye completely at rest during my examination. If I do, then very often the person's vision remains a little blurred for several hours but soon everything goes back to the way it was."

Susan wiggled on her chair. "Well, I'm glad you didn't do it to me," she decided.

27

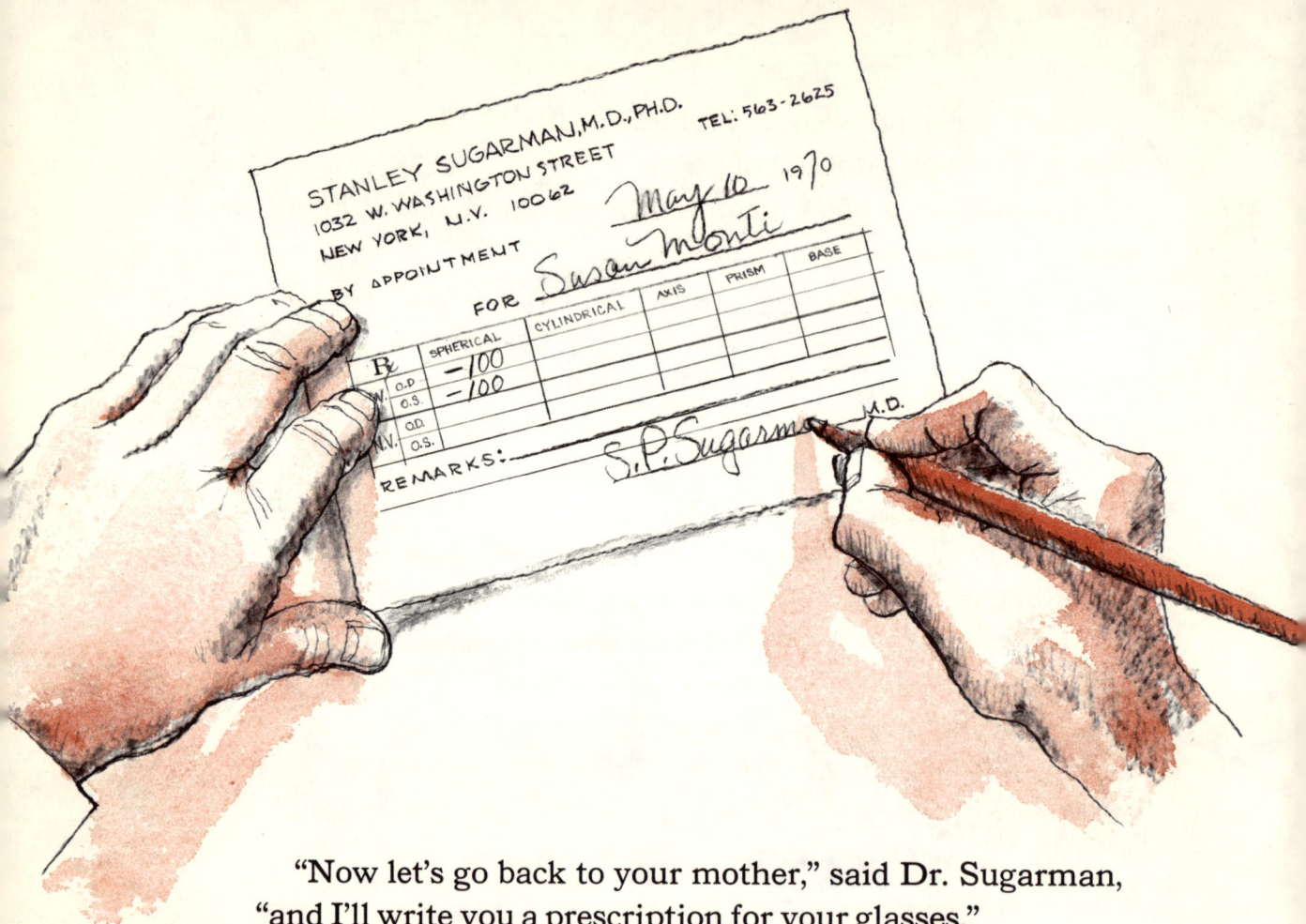

STANLEY SUGARMAN, M.D., PH.D. TEL: 563-2625
1032 W. WASHINGTON STREET
NEW YORK, N.Y. 10062   May 10 1970
BY APPOINTMENT   Susan Monti

FOR Susan

R		SPHERICAL	CYLINDRICAL	AXIS	PRISM	BASE
	O.D	-100				
	O.S.	-100				
	O.D.					
	O.S.					

REMARKS: _____ S. P. Sugarman M.D.

"Now let's go back to your mother," said Dr. Sugarman, "and I'll write you a prescription for your glasses."

"I always thought a prescription was for medicine," said Susan.

"That's true. Doctors prescribe what will help their patients," said Dr. Sugarman, "but it isn't always medicine. When you wear your glasses, you will be able to see better."

He handed a slip of paper to Susan's mother. "Any optician in your neighborhood will make these glasses for Susan," he said. "If your optician has any questions, please have him call me."

"I wonder what I'll look like with glasses," said Susan.

"You'll look very, very pretty," answered the doctor. "If you take a look at the fashion magazines, you'll see that some of the prettiest models wear glasses. So many boys and girls wear glasses that a whole new fashion field has opened up."

"Do I have to wear my glasses all the time?" asked Susan. She was thinking of Jamie.

"It would be a good idea," answered the doctor. "Then, you'll be able to see clearly all the time."

"What's wrong with my eyes?" Susan wanted to know.

"You're near-sighted," said Doctor Sugarman. "Many children are far-sighted and some have other problems, but you are near-sighted and you have trouble seeing far-away objects."

"Why?" asked Susan.

"That's a good question." Dr. Sugarman took a brown paper bag out of his bottom drawer. "Have a peppermint," he said to Susan. "I'll try to answer your question. You see, your eyes work like a camera. The amount of light that passes through the lens of a camera determines whether a picture will be too dark or too light or just right. The iris of the eye controls the amount of light entering the eyeball."

"I know what the eyeball is," interrupted Susan. "But what's an iris?"

"The iris is the colored part of your eye," explained the doctor. "It's called the iris after the Greek goddess of the rainbow."

Susan smiled. "I love stories about gods and goddesses."

"Let Doctor Sugarman continue," said Mrs. Monti. "I'm sure he has patients waiting."

"Your eye has a lens, just like a camera," the doctor went on. "In the center of the iris is a round opening called the pupil. Right behind it is an elastic lens, which is attached to muscles and tissues."

"Oh," said Susan blankly.

Dr. Sugarman got up and went to one of the many bookcases that lined his study. He pulled out a cardboard chart.

"Look at these diagrams," he said. "They will help you to understand what I am talking about."

LENS
RETINA

CORNEA
LIGHT RAYS

PUPIL
IRIS

OPTIC NERVE

SCHEMATIC DRAWING OF A CROSS SECTION OF THE EYE

Susan looked over the doctor's shoulder.

"When the light is dim," said the doctor, "the pupil opens wide and lets in more light. When the light is bright, the pupil opens less widely and not as much light is let in."

Susan was still sucking her peppermint. "I think I understand," she said.

"Good," said the doctor. "Now, when you want to see something far away, the lens muscles of your eyes relax and the lenses thin out for just a second, while your eyes see the object. When you want to see something nearby, the lens muscles contract—the opposite of relax—and the lenses become thicker.

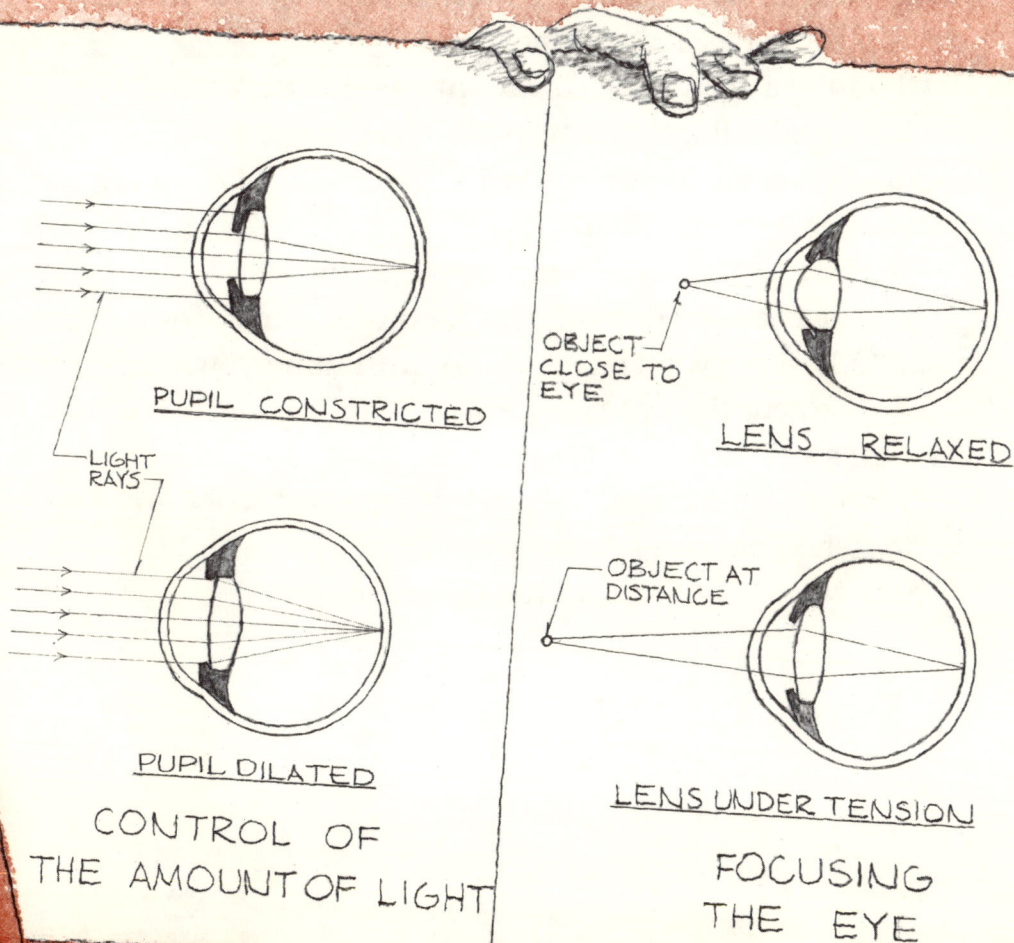

PUPIL CONSTRICTED

LIGHT RAYS

PUPIL DILATED

CONTROL OF THE AMOUNT OF LIGHT

OBJECT CLOSE TO EYE

LENS RELAXED

OBJECT AT DISTANCE

LENS UNDER TENSION

FOCUSING THE EYE

"When a person is near-sighted, like you, she can see nearby objects better than she can those that are far away. Then I prescribe lenses that spread the light rays and help the lenses of your eyes bring far-away objects closer."

"And if a person is far-sighted, everything you told me is just the opposite?" asked Susan.

"That's right," said the doctor. "Next time you come, we'll talk again. Please wear your glasses all the time and come back to see me in six months. My nurse will send you a postcard as a reminder."

"Thank you for being so patient," said Mrs. Monti.

"I enjoyed talking to Susan," said Dr. Sugarman.

Susan waved to Jamie on her way out. "I'm going to get glasses, too," she said.

On the way home the bus was very crowded.

"I hope the optician will still be there," Mrs. Monti worried. "Otherwise we'll have to wait until tomorrow."

Mr. Crown, the optician, was still in his store. He was putting away lenses and frames.

"It's just six o'clock," he said, "but you can be my last customer. What can I do for you?"

Mrs. Monti handed him the prescription.

"So Susan needs glasses," said Mr. Crown. "Let's find you a frame first."

He showed Susan a tray with frames. "All these will fit a pretty girl like you," he said. "Try this pink frame."

Susan looked in the mirror with the empty frame on her nose.

"It feels tight," she said.

"This blue one looks wider," said her mother. "Besides, blue is a good color for you."

The blue frame fit perfectly. "It doesn't rub at all," said Susan.

"That's the one, then," said Mr. Crown. "If you come back Thursday afternoon, I'll have your lenses."

Susan and her mother walked home very quickly.

"Why does it take so long to get the lenses?" asked Susan.

"Mr. Crown orders them from a factory," explained her mother. "He has to wait for their delivery. Then he fits them into your frame and you can pick them up."

Susan could hardly wait for Thursday afternoon.

"Right on time," said Mr. Crown. "Your glasses just came. I gave you shatterproof lenses. All the children wear those."

Susan tried on her new glasses. She looked at herself in the mirror that was standing on the table. Then she glanced at some of the magazines lying on the table. Every page showed a beautiful girl wearing glasses.

"Am I going to have sunglasses, too?" she asked her mother.

"What do you think?" Mrs. Monti looked at the optician.

Mr. Crown was bending Susan's earpieces. "You don't need prescription sunglasses unless you're going to the beach this summer," he said. "Sunglasses should be worn only in very bright sunlight or when there's a real glare— when the water reflects the sun."

"We'll come back in the summer," said Mrs. Monti.

"Fine," said Mr. Crown. He put Susan's glasses back on her nose. "Be sure the earpieces don't rub," he said. "If they aren't comfortable, stop by and I'll adjust them for you any time."

"You look so pretty," said Mrs. Monti to Susan. "And the color of the frame matches your eyes."

Mr. Crown gave Susan a case for her glasses. "Always put them in here during the night," he said, "and don't leave your glasses with the lenses face down or you'll scratch them." He handed Susan a cloth for wiping her glasses. "Keep them clean," he advised. "They are your own private windows, and dirty windows are annoying."

Susan giggled. "My own windows! I never thought of it that way."

The next day in school all the children looked at Susan.

"May I sit in my old seat?" she asked Mrs. Johnson.
"I have my own private windows, and I am sure I can see
the board."

"We'll try it," said Mrs. Johnson.

Susan moved back to the last row, with Ellen and Lisa.

Gg Hh Ii Jj Kk

"Read the numbers on the board," said the teacher. "Seven, eleven, fourteen," Susan read clearly and surely.

"Right," said the teacher. "You may stay back there as long as there is no talking. After all, glasses are for seeing and not for whispering."

39

Susan nodded. "Glasses are fun," she said. "They make the whole world look brighter."

"I bet you'll be able to jump rope now," whispered Ellen.

"Sure," said Susan, "and you can be the monkey in the middle!"